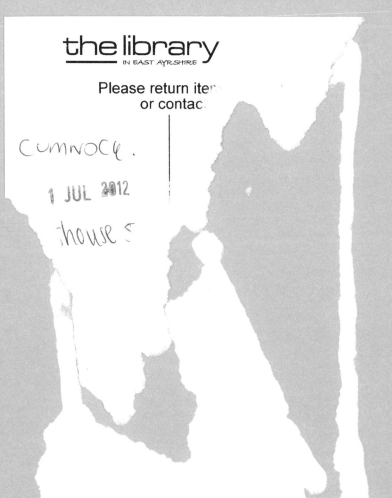

THE STORY OF

Coca-Cola

First published in the UK in 2011 by
Franklin Watts
338 Euston Road
London NW1 3BH

Franklin Watts Australia
Level 17/207 Kent Street
Sydney, NSW 2000

First published by Creative Education, an imprint of The
Creative Company.

A CIP catalogue record for this book is available from the
British Library.

ISBN: 978 1 4451 0595 6

Dewey number: 338.7'66362

Printed in China

Franklin Watts is a division of
Hachette Children's Books,
an Hachette UK company.

www.hachette.co.uk

DESIGN AND PRODUCTION BY **ZENO DESIGN**

PHOTOGRAPHS BY Alamy (Steve Cavalier, Ian Dagnall, Joan
Gamell Farré , Peter Horree, INTERFOTO Pressebildagentur,
Andre Jenny, Tom Mackie, Jenny Matthews, The Natural
History Museum, Walter Pietsch), ASSOCIATED PRESS,
Corbis (Bettmann, Kevin Fleming, Josh Westrich/zefa), Getty
Images (Blank Archives, Margaret Bourke-White//Time Life
Pictures, Hulton Archive, Rod Long, George Marks, M&C
Saatchi Sport & Entertainment, Justin Sullivan)

BUILT FOR SUCCESS

THE STORY OF

Coca-Cola

W

FRANKLIN WATTS
LONDON • SYDNEY

VALERIE BODDEN

Every second of every day, people around the globe pop open a Coca-Cola product. It all adds up to more than 1.7 billion Coca-Cola products being consumed every day! With people in over 200 countries drinking Coca-Cola, it's no wonder the soft drink has become the world's most valuable brand – and the most recognised product on the planet. Relying on clever advertising, catchy slogans and a connection with people around the world, the Coca-Cola Company today earns £15 billion ($24 billion) a year selling over 3,500 different products, including soft drinks, juices, teas, sports drinks and bottled water. Yet the world's largest non-alcoholic beverage producer is still known best for its namesake and the product that got it all started more than one century ago: Coca-Cola.

CHAPTER ONE

Discovering Coca-Cola

When John Pemberton, a **chemist** from Atlanta, Georgia, USA, began to mix together the ingredients that would later become Coca-Cola, his intention was not to create a soft drink at all but a **tonic** for headaches. Working in the back of his shop in 1886, Pemberton mixed fruit syrup, **extracts** of the cola nut and the coca leaf, and other ingredients in a three-legged brass pot, stirring and heating them until they formed a sticky brown syrup.

After sampling his tonic, Pemberton decided to take it to Jacobs' Pharmacy, the largest chemist in Atlanta, where the manager agreed to mix it with water and sell it at his in-store soda fountain for 3p (five cents) a glass.

Before the new drink could be promoted, however, it needed a name and Pemberton's business partner Frank Robinson suggested 'Coca-Cola' as he thought the two Cs would look good in advertisements. He carefully penned the beverage's name in flowing script – the same that is used today – and the partners placed their first ad for the drink in *The Atlanta Journal*, proclaiming that Coca-Cola was "Delicious! Refreshing! Exhilarating! Invigorating!".

Many early Coca-Cola advertisements aimed to create an image that was both classy and casual.

As Jacobs' Pharmacy continued to sell Coca-Cola, someone added **carbonated (fizzy) water** to the drink in place of tap water (whether intentionally or not, no one knows), and customers who tried the new bubbly drink liked it even better. Soon Coca-Cola was being sold as a fizzy drink in soda fountains around Atlanta. In addition to continued advertising in the form of hand-painted Coca-Cola signs at chemists, Pemberton and Robinson began to issue vouchers for free samples of the drink as a way to get customers to try it. Although many liked the new cola drink, sales during the first year were slow, bringing the partners only £30 ($50), which didn't even cover the £50 ($75) in expenses they had spent.

Soon Pemberton's health began to deteriorate and he decided to sell **shares** of his business to his partners. In 1888, shortly before he died, Pemberton sold his last remaining share to an Atlanta doctor and chemist called Asa G Candler. By 1891, Candler had bought out the other people who owned shares of the business, spending a total of £1,430 ($2,300), and he formed the Coca-Cola Company the next year.

Because soda fountain operators often complained that the original formula for Coca-Cola spoiled, Candler quickly set out to change the syrup. In addition to improving the product, Candler also put a heavy emphasis on promoting it. Besides continuing Pemberton's tradition of distributing free drinks vouchers, he created banners, calendars, serving trays, posters, clocks, paper fans and other items, all bearing the Coca-Cola name.

As a result of Candler's **marketing** focus, sales of Coca-Cola rose quickly, reaching nearly 189,270 litres (50,000 US gallons) a year by 1893, up from Pemberton's 95 litres (25 US gallons) in 1886. With such a huge increase in sales, the Coca-Cola Company began to expand, opening syrup manufacturing plants in Dallas, Texas, in 1894 and in Chicago, Illinois, and Los Angeles, California, in 1895. By then, Coca-Cola was being sold in every state and territory of the USA. Despite Coca-Cola's widespread popularity, people could buy the product only at

Soda fountains, popular gathering places in the early 1900s, drove much of Coca-Cola's early success soda fountains; there was no way for them to bring it home. This was to change in 1894 when a Mississippi soda fountain operator called Joseph Biedenharn set up a bottling machine in his shop, becoming the first person to bottle the drink. When Biedenharn sent a case of the bottled soft drink to Candler, Candler pronounced it "fine" but took no further action.

Then, in 1899, Candler was again approached with the idea of bottling Coca-Cola when two lawyers from Tennessee, Benjamin Thomas and Joseph Whitehead, asked him for exclusive rights to bottle and sell the drink. Candler granted their request and the two men soon joined with John Lupton, another Tennessee lawyer, and began to set up their bottling business. Because there was no way for the three men to bottle enough Coca-Cola to supply the whole country themselves, they sold bottling rights to independent bottlers. Within 10 years, nearly 400 plants were bottling Coca-Cola; that number soon increased to 1,000. Throughout the early 1900s, bottling plants were even established outside the US in such places as Cuba, Panama, Canada and Puerto Rico.

However, even as it was expanding, the Coca-Cola Company was also dealing with some troubling issues, as people began to claim that Coca-Cola's use of the coca leaf meant that it contained **cocaine**. In 1901, Candler issued a pamphlet revealing that a study had found only a trace amount of cocaine in the syrup, an amount "so small that it would be simply impossible for anyone to form the cocaine habit from drinking Coca-Cola". Even so, soon after releasing the pamphlet, Candler charged a chemist with the task of removing the cocaine from the syrup, which was accomplished by 1905.

Despite the negative publicity surrounding the presence of cocaine in the drink, sales continued to climb, fuelled by a huge advertising budget that made Coke (as the product was often called) the best advertised item in America. In 1904, the company sold a record 3.8 million litres (1 million US gallons); by 1910, it was selling more than 15 million litres (4 million US gallons) a year. Coca-Cola was well on its way to becoming the world's favourite soft drink.

> "Coca-Cola is...a sublimated essence of all that America stands for, a decent thing, honestly made."
>
> WILLIAM ALLEN WHITE, NEWSPAPER EDITOR

D.Blair ad nat.del.et lith.

M&N Hanhart imp.

ERYTHROXYLON COCA, *Lam.*

The tropical coca plant is the source of both an important Coca-Cola ingredient and the drug cocaine

THE SODA FOUNTAIN

Beginning in the early 1800s, soda fountains could be found in chemists (or 'drugstores') across America. In many small towns soda fountains were gathering places where people could socialise while enjoying a cool soft drink or light snack such as a sandwich or ice-cream sundae. Early soda fountain flavours included orange, lemon, sarsaparilla, berry, ginger ale and root beer. As with Coca-Cola, the drinks were made of flavoured syrup mixed with fizzy water. After they ordered their drink, customers could mingle at the soda fountain's bar or enjoy their own private table, sometimes surrounded by tall plants that provided extra privacy. Many soda fountains were luxuriously decorated, with marble counters, tiled floors and high ceilings. The actual fountains, or syrup dispensers, were also ornate structures, some reaching more than 1.5 metres (5 ft) high. Many were adorned with elaborately carved animals and their marble bases were surrounded by taps to dispense the flavoured syrup.

CHAPTER TWO

Worldwide growth

Because of its great success, Coca-Cola soon found the **market** flooded with hundreds of imitation soft drinks including King Cola, Cola Ree, Cold Cola, Koca-Nola and Ko-Kola. In order to defend its **trademarked** product, the company began to sue such imitators in 1906.

One case in particular, against the Koke Company of America, dragged on for years and was taken all the way to the US Supreme Court, which declared in 1920 that Coca-Cola was "a single thing coming from a single source, and well known to the community", and that Koke was a fraud and could no longer be sold under the sound-alike name.

As it battled imitators the Coca-Cola Company also found a unique way to make its product stand out from the others. In 1916, the company began using a new bottle. Instead of the straight sides found on all other soft drinks bottles, the new Coca-Cola bottle featured contoured sides, making it recognisable by feel alone. In fact, the design was so unique that 60 years later the US Patent Office granted it trademark status, making it one of the few packages ever to be trademarked.

Despite Coca-Cola's continuing success, in 1916, Asa Candler decided to leave the company to serve as Atlanta's mayor. In his place, his son Charles Howard Candler assumed leadership of the company. A year later, in October 1917, Coca-Cola found

Coca-Cola's sloping lettering and unique bottle design helped separate it from its many imitators itself facing a near-crisis as the US government – which had entered World War One in April – declared that sugar would be **rationed**. As sugar was one of the main ingredients in its product, the Coca-Cola Company was hit hard. "We are finding it exceedingly difficult to secure sufficient amounts of sugar and other materials to keep our plants running, and even where we are able to obtain raw materials, it is at such prices that practically eliminate all profits," Sam Dobbs, the company's vice president and manager of sales and advertising, wrote to one of his salesmen. Although the sugar shortage put many soft drinks companies out of business, Coca-Cola survived; when sugar restrictions were removed in 1919, sales of the product boomed.

The year 1919 also saw new ownership of the Coca-Cola Company when a group of investors led by Atlanta banker Ernest Woodruff bought it for £16 million ($25 million). Woodruff and his partners immediately offered **stock** in the company to the public. Although the stock sold quickly Coca-Cola was soon facing trouble again. Following the sugar rationing of World War One, sugar prices began to rise steeply, reaching 17p per 0.45 kilogram (28 cents per pound) in 1920. Fearing that prices would continue to skyrocket, Charles Howard Candler (who continued to serve as chairman) made a deal with sugar suppliers to purchase six months' worth of sugar for 17p per 0.45 kg. Then, shortly after the deal was made, sugar prices fell dramatically to 6p per 0.45 kg (10 cents per pound). The Coca-Cola Company was now stuck with huge amounts of overpriced sugar. Sparked by this crisis, Coca-Cola soon created a new ad campaign with the slogan "Thirst Knows No Season" in an attempt to get people to consume their drink – typically considered a summer refreshment – year-round. The campaign worked and soon the overpriced sugar was gone.

In April 1923, the Coca-Cola Company again faced change as Woodruff's son Robert Winship Woodruff was elected president. He quickly instituted a new quality training programme to establish standards for selling Coca-Cola at soda fountains and in bottles, ensuring that no matter where – or in what form – a

> "[The story of Coca-Cola] is a story of the power of men and money to control what you think, to generate a blend of images that captivate your imagination, that will make you think 'Coke'."
>
> BOB HALL, JOURNALIST

Sugar rationing during World War One was closely monitored, limiting Coca-Cola's production

COCA-COLA

customer purchased a Coca-Cola, it would always taste the same. In addition to guaranteeing the quality of Coca-Cola, Woodruff also wanted to make the product easier to purchase.

In 1923, the company introduced the six-bottle carton, meaning that consumers now had the option of purchasing something besides single bottles or heavy wooden crates of the soft drink. In the late 1920s, Coca-Cola also introduced its first vending machine, consisting of a chest of ice filled with Coke. Although this model still required customers to pay an attendant before taking a Coke, in the early 1930s, coin-operated vending machines began to appear.

Even as these innovations began to boost sales of Coca-Cola in America, the company set in motion a structured programme to distribute Coke around the world. In 1920, a company in France became the first European bottler of Coca-Cola and, in 1926, Woodruff created the Foreign Department (which later became the Coca-Cola Export Corporation) to continue Coca-Cola's spread across the globe. In 1928, Coca-Cola was introduced to people from around the world when it was served at the Olympic Games in Amsterdam.

Part of the reason for the Coca-Cola Company's continued expansion during these years was once again its focus on advertising as Woodruff sought to make Coca-Cola a part of everyone's daily life. By sponsoring radio programmes, painting its name on walls and billboards, and splashing its ads across newspaper and magazine pages, Coca-Cola was able to lay claim to two thirds of the American drinks market, as well as a growing share of the market in other parts of the world. Even during the **Great Depression**, Coca-Cola sales remained fairly strong, as people could always find 3p (5 cents) for a Coke.

のどからハッピー
ここからハッピー

Refreshing & Uplifting

¥120 ¥120 ¥120 ¥120 ¥120

Vending machines, simplistic and rare in the 1930s, are today found in their millions throughout the world

SANTA'S NEW LOOK

As unlikely as it may seem, Coca-Cola's advertisements have influenced not only how people think of the soft drink but also how they think of Father Christmas, or Santa Claus. In 1931, Coca-Cola decided to use the image of Father Christmas in its Christmas ad campaign. The only problem was that, at that time, there were many different images of Father Christmas. Some pictured him as a jolly elf; others portrayed him as tall and thin. In order to solve this problem, the Coca-Cola Company hired artist Haddon Sundblom to paint a new Father Christmas for its ads. The Santa he created was chubby and cheerful, with a white beard and round, red cheeks, a red suit – and, of course, he enjoyed Coca-Cola. Today Sundblom's image of Father Christmas (with or without the Coke) is the one that comes to mind when most people think about Santa.

CHAPTER THREE

Going to war

On 7 December 1941, the Japanese bombed the US naval base at Pearl Harbor, Hawaii, drawing America into World War Two. By that time, Coca-Cola was being bottled in 44 countries, many of them US **allies** and some of them – such as Germany – US enemies. With America's entry into the war, Robert Woodruff ordered the company "to see that every man in uniform gets a bottle of Coca-Cola for five cents [3p], wherever he is and whatever it costs the company."

Even as the company was gearing up to fulfill Woodruff's directive, in 1943 a message arrived from General Dwight Eisenhower, the commander of the Allied forces in Europe. Eisenhower requested that the company send the materials needed for 10 bottling plants, along with three million filled bottles of Coke. Eisenhower's request was quickly granted, and soon Coca-Cola bottling plants were set up close to Allied forces throughout Europe and the Pacific; some of the plants were even portable and followed the advancing armies. 'Technical Observers' from the company delivered Coke to the soldiers, sometimes facing great danger – three were killed during the course of the war. By the end of hostilities, the company had established 64 new bottling plants overseas.

During World War Two, Coca-Cola was a treasured taste of home for US soldiers on the battle lines

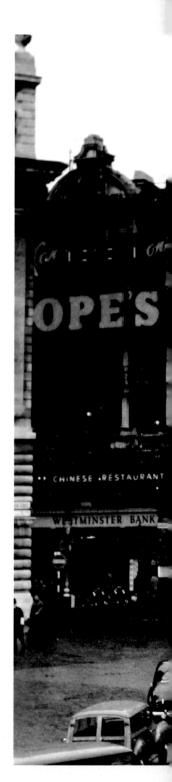

For the grateful soldiers who received the bottled Coca-Cola, the drink wasn't only a way to quench their thirst; it was a reminder of home. As private Dave Edwards wrote to his brother from Italy in 1944, "Today was such a big day that I had to write and tell you about it. Everyone in the company got a Coca-Cola. That might not seem like much to you, but I wish you could see some of these guys who have been overseas for 20 months. They clutch their Coke to their chest, run to their tent and just look at it. No one has drunk theirs yet, for after you drink it, it's gone; so they don't know what to do." With soldiers clamouring for Coca-Cola, more than five billion bottles of the drink were served to military personnel during the war.

Besides providing a taste of home for American soldiers, the new Coca-Cola bottling plants set up during the war introduced local people to the product, opening new markets for growth when the war ended in 1945. Many of the company's wartime bottling plants were converted to peacetime use after the war and, by the early 1950s, more than 25 per cent of Coca-Cola's sales came from overseas. In May 1950, *Time* magazine acknowledged Coca-Cola's worldwide success with a cover story entitled *World and Friend*. The cover of the magazine featured an image of a red Coca-Cola disc serving a bottle of Coke to a happy globe and the text of the article applauded Coca-Cola's efforts to spread the 'American way of life'.

As in the past, Coca-Cola's continued growth also brought with it a strong focus on advertising. During the war, images of defence plant workers enjoying Coca-Cola filled the company's advertisements; after the war, slogans such as "Sign of Good Taste" dominated the ads of the 1950s. During that decade, the Coca-Cola Company also added a new kind of advertising – television sponsorship. During the early years of television, companies would sponsor entire shows; rather than running advertisements, they would weave adverts for their products into the content of the programmes. In 1950, Coca-Cola sponsored its first television show, *The Edgar Bergen and Charlie McCarthy*

By the end of World War Two, Coca-Cola had put down roots in European countries such as the UK

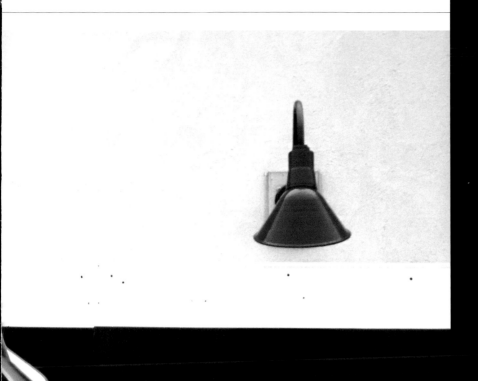

"Your thirst
takes wings

Show, and it later sponsored the musical variety show *Coke Time with Eddie Fisher*. As sponsorship of entire shows eventually gave way to adverts, Coca-Cola began to air advertisements featuring celebrities such as singers Connie Francis and Anita Bryant.

Despite its success following World War Two, Coca-Cola soon found itself entangled in another kind of war: the cola wars. While Pepsi-Cola had been invented around the same time as Coca-Cola, the company had rarely been able to compete with Coke (although during the 1930s Pepsi had done well by offering a 355 ml (12 oz) bottle for the same price as Coca-Cola's 192 ml (6.5 oz) bottle). In 1949, a former Coca-Cola executive assumed leadership at Pepsi, which soon began to emerge as a real Coke competitor.

By adding new bottle sizes and embarking on a huge advertising campaign, Pepsi was able to increase its sales by more than 100 per cent between 1950 and 1955, causing great alarm among the Coca-Cola Company's leadership. In response, Coca-Cola created two new bottle sizes: the 295 ml (10 oz) king-size and 770 ml (26 oz) family-size bottles. The larger bottles were an instant hit, and Coke also increased the size of its drinks at soda fountains. Despite these steps, by the end of the 1950s, Pepsi-Cola had gained more than one third of the US cola market.

With the cola wars in full swing, Robert Woodruff announced in 1955 that he was retiring, having reached the company's mandatory retirement age of 65. Although former newspaper publisher Bill Robinson took over as the company's president, Woodruff remained on the board of directors and served as chairman of the finance committee, where he continued to wield considerable power. In fact, after his retirement, Woodruff moved into an even bigger office in the company's Atlanta headquarters building, where he continued to go every day until he was in his 80s.

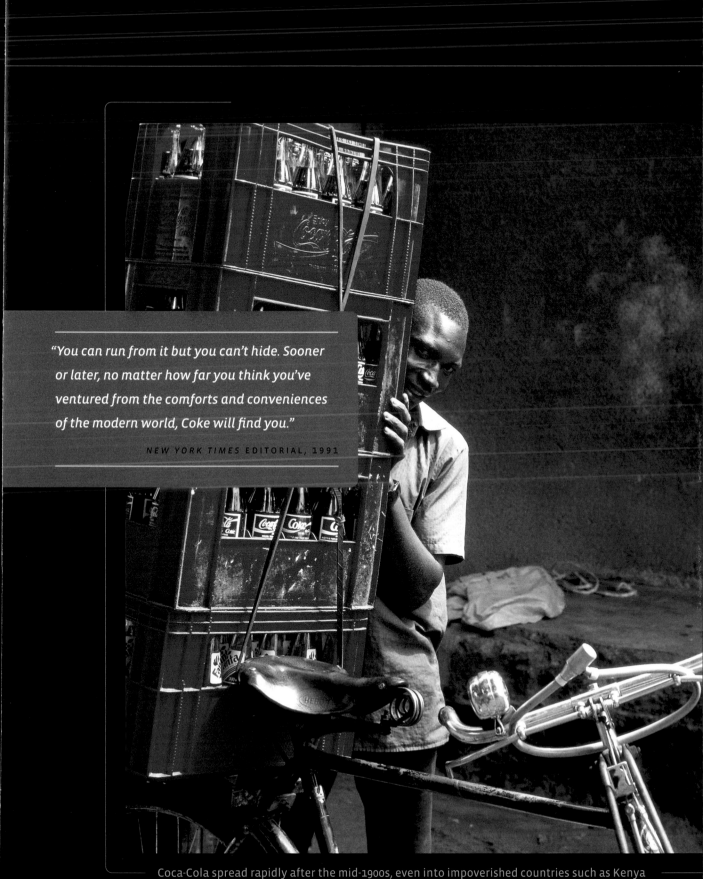

"You can run from it but you can't hide. Sooner or later, no matter how far you think you've ventured from the comforts and conveniences of the modern world, Coke will find you."

NEW YORK TIMES EDITORIAL, 1991

Coca-Cola spread rapidly after the mid-1900s, even into impoverished countries such as Kenya

CHAPTER FOUR

Introducing something new

Until 1960, the Coca-Cola Company sold only one product: Coca-Cola. But that year, the company decided to expand its drink offerings by adding Fanta, a line of fruit-flavoured soft drinks that had been sold by Coke bottlers in other countries for many years, to its drinks list.

Also in 1960, the Coca-Cola Company **acquired** the Minute Maid Corporation and added frozen juice concentrates to its lineup. The next year, the company introduced the citrus-flavoured soft drink Sprite; in 1963, it brought out its first low-calorie fizzy drink called TAB.

While Coca-Cola was introducing its new drinks, Pepsi was introducing a new advertising campaign. With its "Pepsi Generation" ads, Coke's rival tried to convince consumers that Coca-Cola was drunk only by the ageing World War Two generation and that Pepsi was the drink of the young and hip new generation. In response, Coca-Cola came out with the "Things Go Better with Coke" ad campaign, which included radio and television spots featuring different popular music groups such as the Supremes singing a catchy jingle. At a cost of £33 million ($53 million), this campaign made Coca-Cola the most heavily advertised product in the US and helped to keep it ahead of Pepsi in the cola

Pepsi-Cola grew from something of an imitator to a serious Coca-Cola rival in the 1960s and 1970s wars at home, although Pepsi often overtook Coke overseas.

The 1970s saw more innovative ads from Coca-Cola. In 1971, during the Vietnam War, the company released an advert showing young people from across the globe joining together to sing the uplifting song *I'd Like to Buy the World a Coke*. A non-Coke version of the song (entitled *I'd Like to Teach the World to Sing*) soon became a hit. Another popular advert of the 1970s featured a young boy offering a Coke to Pittsburgh Steelers star 'Mean' Joe Greene, causing the burly American football player to smile and toss the boy his jersey.

With Coca-Cola's ads doing so well, Pepsi took a dramatic step in 1975 and introduced the Pepsi Challenge in which the company pitted Pepsi and Coke directly against each other. In a series of blind taste tests, people who reported that they were loyal Coke drinkers repeatedly chose Pepsi over Coke, with the results being aired in Pepsi's television adverts.

As the Pepsi Challenge continued, the Coca-Cola Company promoted Roberto Goizueta, who had begun working for Coke in Havana, Cuba, in 1954, to the position of chief executive to replace Paul Austin, who had served in the position since the 1960s. Goizueta then presided over a series of changes at the company. The first change was the 1982 introduction of Diet Coke (known as Coca-Cola Light in some countries), marking the first extension of the Coca-Cola brand. The new drink was immensely popular and, within two years, it had become the world's best-selling low-calorie soft drink. That same year, Goizueta announced that the company had acquired Columbia Pictures, a film and television production company, for £470 million ($750 million). While many scoffed at the purchase of a company in an unrelated industry, Columbia Pictures proved profitable to Coke and when the company sold it in 1989, it was at a profit of more than £625 million ($1 billion).

Neither the introduction of Diet Coke nor the purchase of Columbia Pictures would make as many headlines as Goizueta's other major change, however. In 1985, worried by the results of the Pepsi Challenge, the Coca-Cola Company

Coca-Cola's advert with American football star Joe Greene, originally aired in 1979, became one of its most famous decided to introduce a new formula for Coca-Cola. Calling their smoother, sweeter formula 'New Coke', the company announced in April 1985, "The best has been made even better." Because blind taste tests had shown that 61 per cent of people preferred New Coke over the original, company leaders were sure their new product would be a success. They were wrong.

What the blind taste tests couldn't show was people's loyalty to the original Coca-Cola. As soon as the new product was announced, the company began to receive calls and letters from angry consumers demanding that the original Coca-Cola be returned to shop shelves. By May, the company was fielding 8,000 calls a day. People began to stockpile supplies of old Coke and some even poured bottles and cans of New Coke into storm drains in protest. A New York newspaper declared that the new beverage was "smoother, sweeter and a threat to a way of life".

In response to the public outcry, Goizueta announced in July that the Coca-Cola Company would reintroduce Coke Classic, telling the American people, "We have heard you." The company's president, Don Keough, said, "The simple fact is that all the time and money and skill poured into consumer research on the new Coca-Cola could not measure or reveal the deep and abiding emotional attachment to original Coca-Cola felt by so many people....The passion for original Coca-Cola – and that is the word for it: passion – was something that caught us by surprise....It is a wonderful American mystery, a lovely American **enigma**, and you cannot measure it any more than you can measure love, pride or **patriotism**."

The day that the change was announced, Coca-Cola received 18,000 calls, this time from grateful consumers. In the following weeks, sales of Coke Classic surged and, by 1986, it had again overtaken Pepsi, which had briefly jumped ahead after the release of New Coke.

"An ice-cold Coke is...a simple pleasure, nothing fancy, offered not to solve the world's problems but to give...a simple moment of satisfaction and refreshment."

DON KEOUGH, FORMER PRESIDENT AND CHIEF
OPERATING OFFICER OF THE COCA-COLA COMPANY

Since the 1985 failure of New Coke, Coca-Cola's original formula has featured the 'classic' label

GUARDING THE FORMULA

Since the early days of Coca-Cola, the beverage's 'secret formula' has been a carefully guarded secret. In addition to sugar, caramel, caffeine, **phosphoric acid**, coca and cola extracts and **glycerin**, the syrup for Coca-Cola contains a secret combination of flavourings and plant extracts that the company mysteriously refers to as Merchandise 7X. The full recipe for the formula is kept in a high-security safety deposit box in the SunTrust Bank in Atlanta, Georgia – legend has it that the box can only be opened if the company's full board of directors votes to open it. In addition, only two senior officials at the company are allowed to know the formula at once and those two officials are reportedly kept from ever travelling on the same aeroplane. The high level of secrecy surrounding the formula has only served to heighten the public's interest in the drink – yet another effective marketing tool employed by the Coca-Cola Company.

CHAPTER FIVE

Refreshing the world

Fortunately for the Coca-Cola Company, the problems with New Coke didn't seem to hurt the company's image around the world. In 1988, three independent surveys found that Coca-Cola was the world's best-known and most admired trademark. A similar survey in 1990 showed that Coke was the most successful brand name in the world.

In order to showcase its success, in 1990, the company opened the World of Coca-Cola museum in Atlanta, which quickly began to attract Coke aficionados. Later in the 1990s, Coca-Cola collectors – who clamour after anything marked with the Coca-Cola logo – flooded new Coca-Cola shops in New York and Las Vegas, where they could purchase everything from vintage Coke postcards to neon Coca-Cola signs.

Throughout the 1990s, Coca-Cola introduced a number of new beverages such as Powerade sports drinks, Fruitopia juices, Planet Java cold coffee drinks and the caffeine-packed Surge citrus soft drink. By the end of the decade, Coca-Cola was selling more than one billion drinks a day, many of them in foreign countries as far-flung as Angola, Afghanistan, China and Mexico.

Fizzy drink options, limited in the mid-1900s, exploded in the 1990s with many new varieties introduced

In 1997, Roberto Goizueta died of lung cancer and, within two years, Doug Ivester, who had taken over as chief executive, found himself facing a crisis. In June 1999, a number of students in Belgium were taken to hospital claiming that Coca-Cola had made them sick. Although there was no evidence that the drinks had caused the illness, Coca-Cola issued an apology and instituted a £155 million ($250 million) product recall. But the damage to the company's image was already done and, in 2000, Ivester was replaced by Douglas Daft, a high-ranking Coca-Cola executive.

One of Daft's first projects as CEO was to preside over a massive restructuring of the company, which involved laying off huge numbers of people – something that had rarely been done in company history. Ultimately, 6,000 people – about 3,300 in the USA and 2,700 overseas – at all levels of the company, from payroll to maintenance, lost their jobs in the corporate shake-up that was intended to make the company more profitable. Also in 2000, the company settled a racial **discrimination** lawsuit that involved more than 2,000 past and current black employees who claimed that the company had long passed over black employees for promotion in favour of white employees, and that white employees routinely received higher pay than black employees. The company offered those involved in the lawsuit £120 million ($192.5 million) and agreed to work towards new diversity goals.

Despite its turbulent start to the new millennium, Coca-Cola continued to introduce new products to its beverage lines. In 2001, Diet Coke with lemon was added; the following year, the company introduced Vanilla Coke. At the same time, sales of Coke's Dasani brand of bottled water, which had been introduced in 1999, began to take off.

After the successful launch of so many products, Daft retired in 2004 and was replaced by E Neville Isdell, a former Coke executive, who came out of retirement to take the position. Under Isdell, the company has continued to introduce new products. Today Coca-Cola offers over 3,500 different drinks around the

A 2000 racial discrimination lawsuit against Coca-Cola stirred up unhappy memories of past prejudice in the USA

Enjoy! Coca-Cola

THE WORLD DRINKS COKE

One of the ways the Coca-Cola Company can tell how popular it is in a certain country is by looking at that country's per capita consumption. Per capita consumption refers to how many 237 millilitre (8 fl oz) servings of Coca-Cola products are consumed by each person in a country in a year (this is found by dividing the number of Coca-Cola products sold by the population of the country). In 2010, per capita consumption of Coca-Cola products ranged from a low of 11 Coca-Cola products per person per year in India to a high of 675 Coca-Cola products per person per year in Mexico. Here's a look at how some other countries compared:

Country	Annual Servings Per Person
China	34
Egypt	54
Russia	69
Morocco	84
France	143
Philippines	144
Japan	178
Great Britain	204
Brazil	229
Canada	236
South Africa	254
Australia	319
United States	394

world. In Chile, consumers can buy Bibo, a snack drink fortified with vitamins. In Australia, young people drink high-energy Burn. In Japan, Coca-Cola's Qoo drink is a best-selling juice brand. In the USA, Enviga, a sparkling green tea reported to help burn calories, was made available in 2007.

With so many beverages being sold in so many countries, the Coca-Cola bottling system is today one of the largest production and distribution systems in the world. As of 2010, the company – including the bottling plants it owns and its associates – employed 139,600 people in over 200 countries. Just as in the past, the Coca-Cola Company today still supplies syrup to its bottling plants, which then mix it with sugar and water, carbonate it, bottle it and ship it. In some countries, the method of shipping can be unique. In Indonesia, boats carry Coca-Cola between islands. In the Amazon, Coca-Cola is floated down the river. And in the Andes Mountains, the drink is often carried by pack animals.

As the Coca-Cola Company moves further into the new millennium, its goal is to keep adding new beverages. "Expanding our beverage portfolio is an important strategic priority," said John Brock, president and chief executive officer (CEO) of Coca-Cola Enterprises, the company's largest bottler. Although the Coca-Cola Company plans to keep soft drinks at its core, increasingly it is looking to roll out new products such as energy drinks, health beverages and vitamin waters. In 2010, for example, the company announced plans to launch VitaminWater stur-D, a blue agave, passion fruit and citrus flavoured drink, the first enhanced water drink to include vitamin D and calcium.

With its focus on new drinks, the Coca-Cola Company has certainly come a long way from that day in 1886 when John Pemberton accidentally discovered Coke's formula. Now chemists regularly (and intentionally) mix ingredients in search of new beverages. And with the Coca-Cola Company's beverages reaching 6 billion of the planet's 6.7 billion people, it looks to be well on its way to refreshing the world.

"Coke's peaceful near-conquest of the world is one of the remarkable phenomena of the age. It has put itself…always within an arm's length of desire."

TIME MAGAZINE ARTICLE, 1950

In recent years, Coca-Cola has unveiled new products, sometimes in partnership with other companies

GLOSSARY

acquired purchased another company

allies nations or groups that are friendly towards one another or that fight together against common enemies in a war

brand the name of a product or manufacturer; a brand distinguishes a product from similar products made by other manufacturers

carbonated (fizzy) water water that has been made bubbly using carbon dioxide

chemist a person who prepares and distributes medicines to the public

cocaine a highly addictive drug made from the leaves of the coca plant

discrimination treating a person or group unfairly because of prejudice; racial discrimination occurs when people are treated unfairly based on their race

enigma something that is difficult to understand; a mystery

extracts concentrated substances that are extracted, or taken out of, their sources such as plants or fruit

glycerin a thick, sweet liquid used in a number of products, including some soft drinks, anti-freeze and cosmetics

Great Depression a time from 1929 to 1939 when there was widespread unemployment in the USA and elsewhere in the world (in the UK from 1929–32), and a major decline in the production and sale of goods

market a geographic region or segment of the population to which companies try to sell goods; for example, the European Union market, the youth market or the world market

marketing advertising and promoting a product in order to increase sales

patriotism to be devoted and ready to support one's own country

phosphoric acid a syrupy acid used in soft drinks, fertilisers and medicines

rationed limited; during times of shortage such as war, governments sometimes set limits on the amount of a product that can be purchased by an individual or company

sarsaparilla a carbonated (fizzy) drink flavoured with the root bark of the sassafras tree and oil from a European birch tree

shares the equal parts a company may be divided into; shareholders each own a certain number of shares, or percentage, of the company

slogans short, attention-grabbing phrases used in advertising

stock shared ownership in a company by many people who buy shares, or portions, of stock, hoping the company will make a profit and the stock value will increase

tonic a mixture designed to refresh and restore people's energy

trademarked registered as belonging legally and exclusively to one company

1886 Chemist John Pemberton invents formula for Coca-Cola, while trying to invent a tonic for headaches

1893 Asa G Candler launches the Coca-Cola Company

1894 Joseph Biedenharn is first person to bottle Coca-Cola

1899 Lawyers Benjamin F Thomas and Joseph B Whitehead purchase rights to bottle and sell Coca-Cola

1900 Coca-Cola is first sold in the UK

1905 The drug cocaine is removed from Coca-Cola following claims that it could make people addicted

1916 Distinctive contour Coca-Cola bottle is introduced

1923 Robert Woodruff becomes company president

1928 Coca-Cola sold at Olympic Games in Amsterdam, the Netherlands

1943 General Eisenhower requests construction of 10 Coca-Cola bottling plants for soldiers during World War Two

1960s Pepsi-Cola becomes Coca-Cola's biggest rival

1971 *I'd Like to Buy the World a Coke* song features in popular advertising campaign

1985 New Coke receives public outcry; Coke Classic appears

2000s Coca-Cola launches health, energy and vitamin drinks

2010 Coca-Cola products drunk globally by 6 billion people

INDEX